Heal the World—Make It A Better Place

Great Quotations Publishing Company

Compiled by Pat Cudimano

© 1993 Great Quotations Publishing Company

Published in the United States by

Great Quotations Publishing Company
1967 Quincy Court
Glendale Heights, IL 60139

Printed in U.S.A.
ISBN: 1-56245-036-0

To those earth-conscious individuals who have helped lower our environmental ignorance.

If we want to make something of this planet, there is nothing whatever that can stop us. We are going to have to find ways to organize ourselves cooperatively, sanely, scientifically and harmonically with the rest of humanity around the earth. Ever since our love for machines replaced the love we used to have for our planet, we have proceeded on to the depletion of our natural resources. This could be such a beautiful world. We hope this book will inspire you to take that next step towards thinking globally. You can make a difference ... at home, in your community, for a better tomorrow.

e stand now where two roads diverge. ...

The one "less traveled by"—offers our last, our only

chance to reach a destination that assures the

preservation of our earth.

Rachel Carson, "Silent Spring"

ecycling one run of the Sunday *New York Times* can save 75,000 trees!

Only one percent of the Earth's water is usable. A running tap puts about three to five gallons of water down the drain per minute. So, stop spending water like money and turn off the tap when not in use.

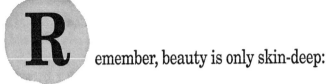

Remember, beauty is only skin-deep: Approximately 60 percent of the pesticides sprayed on fruits and vegetables are applied so that we may have picture-perfect produce.

Cedar acts as a natural moth-repellent when placed in a clothes closet. Some cedar chips placed in a net bag will keep your wardrobe hole-free.

9

An area of tropical rain forest about the size of four city blocks is being destroyed every minute. Burning our rain forests not only kills trees that had once absorbed large quantities of carbon dioxide, it also releases carbon dioxide into the air adding to the greenhouse effect.

We can kick the fossil-fuel habit and reduce our dependency on environmental polluters like oil and coal by converting to renewable energy sources.

The natural beauty of our state parks has refreshed many a weary soul. We can help keep them this way by not littering and by taking home the trash.

Noise has a considerable effect on both our body and mind. It is a primary source of environmental stress, so let's turn down the volume!

The long fight to save wild beauty represents democracy at its best. It requires citizens to practice the hardest of virtues—self-restraint.

Edwin Way Teale, "Circle of Seasons"

Overheating your home is unhealthy because
it dries out the air. You can humidify the house by
lowering the thermostat and placing a few bowls
of water around the house.

Dried herbs make pleasant air-fresheners as well as wonderful seasonings. Herbs also provide food for beneficial insects—try growing a few!

ater is a precious commodity. Take a five-minute

shower instead of a bath and conserve energy and water.

 aste not, want not. The backs of unwanted mail advertisements make great scrap paper for jotting down notes.

A diamond lasts forever—unfortunately so does plastic. Americans currently throw away 15 million tons of plastic a year. It's time to rethink our plastic attraction and stop the environmental abuse.

mericans are world leaders in garbage production. Packaging alone takes up 50 percent of the volume of municipal solid waste.

 **E**cologist Marjorie Lamb's recipe for a greener, healthier planet is, "Reduce, Reuse, Recycle".

e could reduce water consumption by 75 percent
if everyone installed water-saving devices in their homes.

Plants and trees are natural air conditioners. They contribute to our oxygen supply and absorb considerable amounts of carbon dioxide—so why not give a lasting gift and give a green one.

If only one percent of Americans did not use their cars for one day a week, we could save approximately 96 million gallons of gas. Carpooling is an energy-saving option that offers the efficiency of mass transit and some of the flexibility of a private vehicle.

Energy improvements to your home are attractive investment opportunities that make long-term economic sense.

Man thinks of himself as a creator instead of a user, and this delusion is robbing him, not only of his natural heritage, but perhaps of his future.

Helen Hoover, "The Waiting Hills"

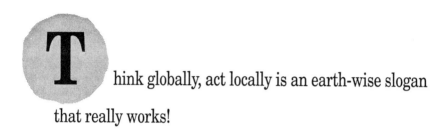 **T**hink globally, act locally is an earth-wise slogan that really works!

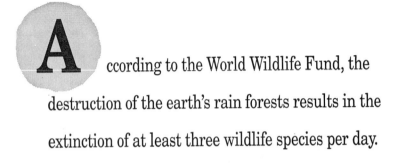

ccording to the World Wildlife Fund, the

destruction of the earth's rain forests results in the

extinction of at least three wildlife species per day.

nergy-efficient appliances use as much as

50 percent less energy than conventional models.

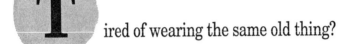 ired of wearing the same old thing?

Try a clothes swap with family or friends and

create an exciting new wardrobe.

One ton of recycled paper saves 17 trees, 7,000 gallons of water, three cubic yards of landfill space, and prevents 60 pounds of pollution from contaminating the air.

Wake up and smell the coffee. Bleached paper filters release the toxic chemical dioxin. Reusable cotton coffee filters are a natural alternative. Or if that's not your cup of tea ... unbleached coffee filters are available at most markets.

By teaching our children the importance of energy conservation today, we insure a brighter tomorrow for our planet.

33

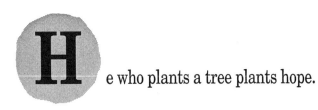

He who plants a tree plants hope.

Lucy Larcom

The transportation of imported foods increases pollution and uses valuable fuel. You can make a difference by shopping at nearby stores that purchase local produce.

Saving the planet has never been an issue of money, but rather a matter of resourcefulness and motivation of individuals.

Spencer Beebe

Environmentally safe baking soda is a terrific all-purpose cleaner. From kitchens to bathrooms, it cleans without polluting.

Disposable diapers not only waste valuable landfill space, but it takes one billion trees per year to manufacture them and they require lifetimes to decompose.

**R**esponsibility starts here: Contamination

of the earth's water system is "our" problem not "theirs".

 ach year, the world deposits 20 billion tons of untreated waste into our oceans.

eaks in pipes and taps are major water wasters. So, until you have time to make necessary repairs, turn off the shut-off valve and place a bucket under the leak.

ive your creative talents a whirl and try mending old clothes with decorative patches.

In 1990, Americans sold more than two million solar calculators. Solar-powered calculators save on disposable batteries which use 50 times more power to make than they generate.

rash the junk. Join the over one million people
who have asked the Direct Marketing Association to
remove their names from junk mail mailing lists.

Touch the earth, love the earth, honour the earth, her plains, her valleys, her hills, and her seas; rest your spirit in her solitary places.

Henry Beston, "Orion Rises on the Dunes"

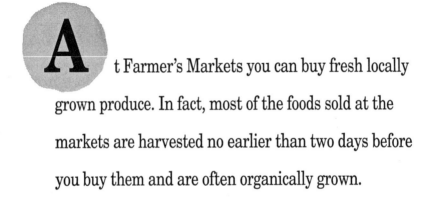

At Farmer's Markets you can buy fresh locally grown produce. In fact, most of the foods sold at the markets are harvested no earlier than two days before you buy them and are often organically grown.

Ozone-depleting CFCs escape into the atmosphere every time refrigerators and air conditioners are improperly discarded. So, start the drive for a "CFC Roundup" program in your community.

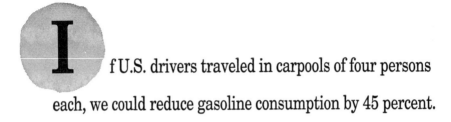

If U.S. drivers traveled in carpools of four persons each, we could reduce gasoline consumption by 45 percent.

Streams and creeks are vital parts of our ecosystem. Take an active role in keeping the environment clean and persuade your organization, community, or school to adopt a stream—let's keep it flowing!

 e do not inherit the land from our ancestors;

we borrow it from our children.

Native American Proverb

You have the power to change your environment. Consumer letters to McDonald's helped phase out unnecessary packaging. And, consumer concerns persuaded Starkist tuna to become "dolphin-safe".

Recycling allows us to conserve natural resources and energy; it significantly contributes to the reduction of pollution; and it helps eliminate the need for more landfills and incineration plants.

Reuse in use: Not only can we learn to buy less, but we can get more use out of the things we do buy. Convert plastic food containers into handy storage containers.

an shapes himself through decisions that shape

his environment.

Rene Dubos

Food for thought: Each year Americans throw away approximately 440 pounds of packaging per person. Foods with the least amount of packaging are both the safest and usually the most economical to buy.

Each year 100,000 marine mammals die from eating or becoming entangled in plastic debris. It's time to hit the beach and clean up our act! Before you discard plastic cut it up into small pieces.

In remaking the world in the likeness of a steam-heated, air-conditioned metropolis of apartment buildings, we have violated one of our essential attributes—our kinship with nature.

Ross Parmenter, "Inward Sign"

s soils are depleted, human health, vitality and intelligence go with them.

Louis Bromfield

Instead of plastic bags, use a cloth or string bag to tote your groceries home. Most markets offer a colorful selection of reusable carry-alls.

By joining an organic food co-op, you can purchase
chemical-free foods in bulk. Buying in bulk also makes
great economic sense and often requires less packaging.

urt not the earth, neither the sea, nor the trees.

Revelation 7:3

he only means of conservation is innovation.

Peter Drucker

Before you can it, remember that church organizations and charities like Goodwill and the Salvation Army are always in need of used clothing and furniture.

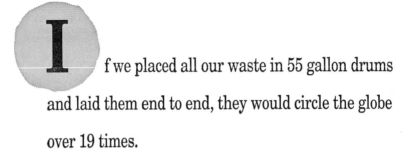

If we placed all our waste in 55 gallon drums and laid them end to end, they would circle the globe over 19 times.

eftover organic kitchen scraps can be used to start a compost pile. When decomposed, the resulting nutrient-rich humus will give an extra boost to any garden.

A grateful environment is a substitute for happiness. It can quicken us from without as a fixed hope and affection, or the consciousness of a right life, can quicken us from within.

George Santayana, "The Sense of Beauty"

e can all make a difference... In 1990, 20/20
Vision led a campaign that diverted $46 million from the
MX Missile Program into a fund for cleaning up toxic
waste at military bases.

ne man's garbage is another man's treasure.
Earn some extra money and recycle your old things by
holding an annual garage sale.

Heat pumps are two to three times more efficient than electric heating systems and can save you up to 50 percent on annual heating costs. Many utility companies offer low-cost financing to customers who want to make the energy-saving switch.

The power that makes grass grow, fruit ripen, and guides the bird in flight is in us all.

Anzia Yezierska

Motor oil can be re-refined to remove dirt so it can be used again. Check your area gas stations to see if they observe recycling practices.

For every gallon of gas a car burns, it puts 18 to 20 pounds of carbon dioxide into the atmosphere. Greenpeace Action reports, "cars are the biggest source of greenhouse gases and the largest cause of ozone smog".

y the mid 1990s, wind power promises to be

among the least expensive sources of electricity.

diaper service is a terrific gift for new parents and is easier on the environment than disposable diapers.

The ozone layer shields us against harmful ultraviolet radiation. However, three to five percent of this layer has already been destroyed by harmful CFCs. You can help protect our ozone layer by purchasing products in pump sprayers instead of CFC-propelled aerosols.

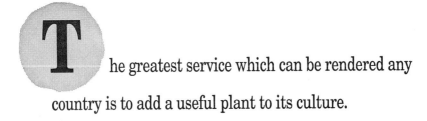

he greatest service which can be rendered any country is to add a useful plant to its culture.

Thomas Jefferson

Environmental protection starts at home. Why not organize a home-based competition that will reduce your family's garbage output in half.

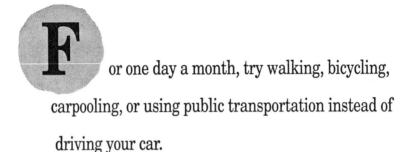

or one day a month, try walking, bicycling, carpooling, or using public transportation instead of driving your car.

orth Americans are the biggest users of fresh water with each person consuming about 53 gallons per day in the home.

The earth we abuse and the living things we kill will, in the end, take their revenge; for in exploiting their presence we are diminishing our future.

Marya Mannes, "More in Anger"

Cut down on paper use by designing home made greeting cards made from a collage of magazines, old greeting cards, and advertisements.

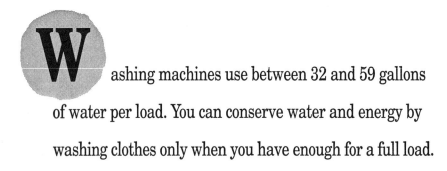 ashing machines use between 32 and 59 gallons of water per load. You can conserve water and energy by washing clothes only when you have enough for a full load.

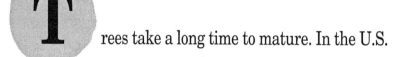rees take a long time to mature. In the U.S. alone, we lose an acre of forest every five seconds.

hen clothes get too worn for wear, cut them into

cleaning rags and save on paper towels.

t the present rate of water consumption, some main groundwater supplies may not last more than 50 years.

Used motor oil contains harmful contaminates. Every year oil equal to 41 Exxon Valdez spills is improperly discarded. The poisons in the oil pollute our water supply, therefore dispose of them at special toxic waste collection sites.

Fuel consumption increases by 20 percent when you raise the speed limit from 55 to 70 m.p.h. The increase also causes a considerable rise in air pollution.

Replace incandescent light bulbs with energy-efficient fluorescent bulbs. Although they are initially more expensive, fluorescent bulbs consume only one-fifth the energy of an ordinary bulb and last approximately 15 times longer.

88

Each year cities and telephone companies provide recycling depots for telephone directories. Phonebooks can be recycled to make record albums and CD covers.

 ave our rainforests and avoid purchasing items
made of tropical hardwoods such as mahogany, teak,
rosewood, and ebony.

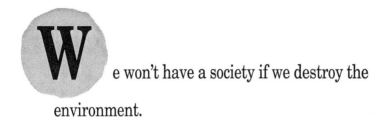 e won't have a society if we destroy the environment.

Margaret Mead

ainwater collected in a barrel could be used to wash the car, water your garden, or give Fido a bath.

A n organic cover of mulch in your garden cuts down on water evaporation and provides extra nutrients to the soil.

e abuse land because we regard it as a commodity belonging to us. When we see land as a community to which we belong, we may begin to use it with love and respect.

Aldo Leopold

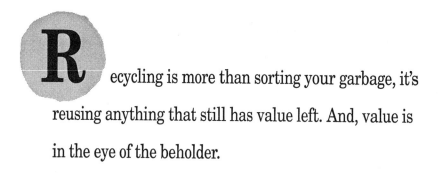

Recycling is more than sorting your garbage, it's reusing anything that still has value left. And, value is in the eye of the beholder.

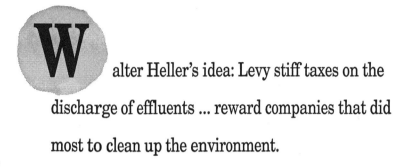

Walter Heller's idea: Levy stiff taxes on the discharge of effluents ... reward companies that did most to clean up the environment.

Time Magazine

The destruction of the rain forest combined with the spread of disease threatens over 1,000 tribes of indigenous people with extinction.

he burning of fossil fuels is the primary cause of the greenhouse effect. Switching to alternatives like solar and wind energy can reduce global warming.

98

When washing clothes, the temperature of the rinse cycle does not affect the cleaning. So, rinse with cold water and reduce your hot-water heating bills.

The recycled difference: "Recycled" products are made either partly or completely of recycled materials. However, "recyclable" means that the products can be recycled if there is some place that will accept them.

When brushing your teeth, you can save about nine gallons of water if you turn on the tap only to wet the brush and to rinse. You can also reduce water heating bills if you wash your hands in cold water.

Here's an old-fashioned drain-cleaning recipe that's sure to put some zip into a sluggish drain.

Pour: Boiling water

Add: 1/2 cup of baking soda
1/2 cup of white vinegar
1/8 cup of salt

ANTED: The Greenhouse Gas Gang

CRIME: Global Warming

Carbon Dioxide	50%
Chlorofluorocarbons (CFCs)	15-20%
Methane	18%
Nitrous Oxides	10%
Ozone (surface-level pollution)	2-5%

reen Cross and Green Seal are two independent

organizations that research and certify products based on

their environmental impact. For more information:

Green Seal
1875 Connecticut Ave., NW, Suite 300 A
Washington D.C. 20009   (Send SASE - Free)

Green Cross Certification Company
Tel# (800) 829-1416 or (510) 832-1415

Over 100 cities have passed laws limiting the use of polystyrene foam (styrofoam). This plastic is not biodegradable, it releases harmful CFCs into the air as it decomposes, and it has been discovered that toxic compounds are produced when this plastic is burned.

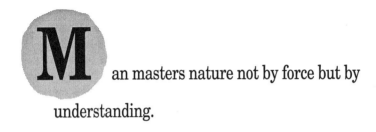 **M**an masters nature not by force but by understanding.

Jacob Bronowski, "The Creative Mind"

Today almost 85 percent of U.S. energy needs are met in one way or another by fossil fuels. Over 60 percent of our energy is supplied by foreign oil. If we don't diversify our energy appetites, we will be at the mercy of OPEC within a few decades.

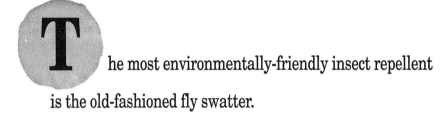 he most environmentally-friendly insect repellent is the old-fashioned fly swatter.

Make the switch: Alternative fuels such as ethanol and gasohol are renewable alternatives made from organic plant matter that is blended with gasoline.

In support of saving the world's rainforests, many companies are using nuts, leaves, and other items harvested in the tropical forest for use in their products. We can help the cause by providing a market for these goods.

Energy conservation and increasing the efficiency of our energy use are the most effective ways to reduce environmental impact.

You can become part of the solution to our environmental problems by using biodegradable, nontoxic cleaning products. These products are phosphate-free, perfume-free, and the containers are made from recycled materials.

When you receive a boxed gift, save the box and reuse it. As the gift box is passed along, try attaching a homemade memento to it. In no time at all, the box will be completely decorated and will no longer need to be wrapped.

More than half the pesticides that we ingest come from meat and dairy products. We can reduce our consumption by eating less meat and by purchasing chemically-free organic produce.

Cast your ballot. Voting locally affects national policies. Many environmental policies get their start at local levels before being adopted by state and federal governments. So get out and vote.

Low-flow faucet aerators on kitchen and bathroom taps can save a family of four over 3300 gallons per year. At about four dollars per aerator, this is an exceptional water-saving buy.

Trees are the earth's endless effort to speak to the listening heaven.

Rabindranath Tagore, "Fireflies"

Excessive pesticide and herbicide spraying affects all of us. In one instance, 1000 wells in Florida had to be closed down because the drinking water had been contaminated with these toxic substances.

118

You could put your money where your environmental concerns lie by supporting stores that carry ecologically-safe products. And, once the demand increases, the prices will begin to decrease.

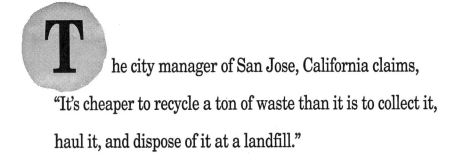

The city manager of San Jose, California claims, "It's cheaper to recycle a ton of waste than it is to collect it, haul it, and dispose of it at a landfill."

Pedal-pushers. The most damaging pollution occurs during the first few minutes that a car is running. So, the next time that you need to take a quick trip around town, use your bike instead of the car and help reduce air pollution.

Growing your own food increases your self-sufficiency and brings you back in touch with the earth. Companion planting and crop rotation practices will help keep your garden pest-free and chemical-free.

The U.S. consumes more energy for air conditioning than the total energy consumption of the 800 million people in China.

Robert O. Anderson

The expense and energy used to process and package food is considerable. And, the waste they produce is often laden with harmful chemicals.

By cutting back on washing your car, you can save as much as 15 gallons of drinkable water per cleaning.

t the office, you can save money and valuable

landfill space by using both sides of the copier paper.

If the prospect for human freedom in the last half of this twentieth century is to become any brighter, we have got to find a better way to develop and use the riches of this earth.

Oscar L. Chapman

You can encourage manufacturers to reduce excess packaging by notifying the company through their customer service, toll-free telephone number that is usually listed on the package.

By just replacing your standard light bulb with a compact fluorescent bulb, you can save the equivalent of 600 pounds of coal over the life of the bulb.

Support the recycling effort by visiting second-hand outlets. Most second-hand shops offer a unique selection of used merchandise like clothes, furniture, and books at very reasonable prices.

Paint contains more than 300 toxic substances and must be disposed of at a hazardous waste facility. As a direct result, some communities have initiated paint exchange programs that help use up leftover paint and save landfill space.

Disposable diapers produce seven times more waste than cloth diapers. Although cloth diapers are less expensive and are biodegradable, Americans continue to favor the disposable at a rate of 18 billion a year.

A Water-Watchdog: If you suspect that a nearby lake, stream, or pond is in danger of being polluted, contact the water-monitoring agency for your area to see how you can help.

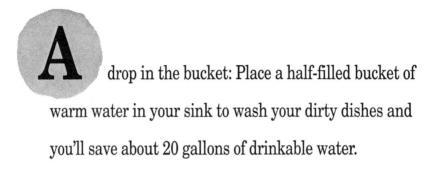 drop in the bucket: Place a half-filled bucket of warm water in your sink to wash your dirty dishes and you'll save about 20 gallons of drinkable water.

Substitute your plastic bags and wrap with biodegradable wax paper. Or, you can purchase biodegradable, nontoxic bags made out of 100% cellulose from the store.

After you mow, leave grass clippings on the ground to naturally fertilize and mulch the lawn. The mulch will prevent water evaporation and will also provide nutrients, thus eliminating the need for extra watering and chemical applications.

cology has become the political substitute for the word "mother".

Jesse Unruh

PTA's are powerful organizations that have played a major role in educating the public. Why not start a "green committee" for your local PTA and address environmental concerns in your community—don't forget to include the kids.

138

Give carpooling a boost at your place of business, by asking employers to provide added incentives such as free parking spaces for those who double-up when driving to the office.

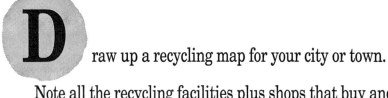raw up a recycling map for your city or town. Note all the recycling facilities plus shops that buy and sell used items. This recycling venture is a great fund raiser and makes ecological sense.

Portable fans are a low-cost alternative to air conditioners and they don't contain harmful CFC's which damage the ozone-layer.

The average American car spews about two tons of carbon into the air each year. These vehicles also produce nitrous oxide which returns to earth as acid rain. Acid rain affects our entire ecosystem, destroying trees, lakes, fish, and wildlife.

 ot Tips:

- By lowering your thermostat just one degree, you can save two percent on your heating bill.

- Furnace tune-ups increase heating efficiency by five percent.

- During the cold weather, change air filters on hot air heating systems every month.

Pets attract fleas but most flea collars on the market are highly toxic and pose long-term health risks for both you and your pet. Herbal mixtures composed of mints, pansy, or garlic and cedar-chip pillows are natural remedies that help keep your pet flea-free.

By installing new water-saving toilets, a family of four can save up to 32,000 gallons of water per year. You can also reduce the amount of water per flush by placing a filled container in the tank. The container displaces some of the water and saves one to two gallons per flush.

It is ironic that in an age when we have prided ourselves on our progress in the intelligent care and teaching of our children we have at the same time put them at the mercy of new and most terrible weapons of destruction.

Pearl S. Buck, "What America Means To Me

Cellulose fiber is made from recycled newspapers. It is easy on the environment and it can be used as insulation in a number of materials.

By reducing our meat consumption by just ten percent, we could save enough grain and soybean to feed 60 million people. Try experimenting with a few vegetarian dishes as a substitute for meat.

IMBY: Not In My Backyard. None of us wish to see a landfill or incinerator plant built in our neighborhood. Yet we still continue building those mounds of garbage. Responsible waste management is essential domestic housekeeping for everyone.

Avoid processed and over-packaged fast foods when on a long family outing. Instead, take time to pack a supply of snack foods and drinks for the journey. Iced water, fresh fruits, raw vegetables, and nuts travel well and are easy to eat.

Lights and appliances like refrigerators generate a considerable amount of heat. You can beat the heat by turning off the lights whenever you leave the room. And refrigerator doors should be kept closed as much as possible.

According to the American Council for an Energy Efficient Economy, "The single most important thing people can do to save energy in their homes is to make sure their furnaces are running efficiently. More energy is used for heating than any other purpose in American apartments and houses."

Put your purchase power to good use and help protect wildlife. Our greed for exotic adornments has led to the extinction of many species of animals. You can help put a halt to the senseless slaughter by refusing to purchase any products made from endangered animals.

Precycling Awareness: Packaging is responsible for about five million tons of garbage each year. By selecting items that contain less packaging, you are putting your precycle practices to work. So when shopping, ask yourself, "Is it recyclable?", "Is it reusable?", Is it good for the environment?"

You can help prevent a brown-out by using heavy energy consuming appliances like dishwashers, washing machines, and dryers during off-peak hours. You can also conserve watts by using hand-held appliances instead of their electric counterparts.

Children are eager supporters of environmental awareness. Teach your children the importance of sound ecological habits by starting a clean-up project in your home, school, or community.

Glass can be recycled over and over again with very little additional material. Recycled glass reduces energy use by up to 32 percent, air pollution by 20 percent, mining wastes by 80 percent, and water use by 50 percent.

Pre-treated lumber often contains poisonous preservatives, fungicides, and insecticides. Cedar is a natural substitute that is rot and insect resistant.

void disposable and one-time use only items. Store leftovers in reusable containers rather than using plastic wrap or aluminum foil. And instead of buying special plastic bags, line your waste baskets with used grocery bags.

We of the age of machines, having delivered ourselves of nocturnal enemies, now have a dislike of night itself. With lights and ever more lights, we drive the holiness and beauty of the night back to the forests and the sea.

Henry Beston, "Night on the Great Beach"

160

Improve on your car's gas mileage with these driving tips:

- Use radial tires.
- Have your tires properly balanced.
- Make sure that your tires are filled with the correct air pressure.
- Drive slower.
- Turn off the air conditioner and open the windows.

**P**et Peeves: Promote recycling by using
biodegradable cat litter made from recycled newspaper.
A little sprinkle of baking soda and periodic cleaning
will keep the litter box fresh without the use of harsh
chemicals.

You can prevent excessive heat-loss during cold winter months by making sure that all doors and windows are well-sealed with caulking or weather stripping. Covering windows with energy-saving blinds or drapes in the evening is also a great heat-saver.

The office is an excellent place to put recycling measures and waste management controls to the test.

Here are a few user ideas:

- Start a recycling bin for used computer and copier paper.
- Bring a ceramic mug to work to replace styrofoam cups.
- Rather than wasting paper, use electronic mail to send memos.

Judging from the mounds of garbage overflowing in our landfills, it is obvious that we live in a throw-away society. So why not give your fix-it talents a try and repair items before you trash them.

In the last few years, commuters wasted three billion gallons of gas and spent two billion hours in traffic jams. This is enough fuel to drive to the sun and back more than 300 times!

Give those shower-lovers on your gift list a water-saving shower head. When installed, these devices will not only reduce water consumption by 50 to 75 percent, they can also lower waste-heating bills dramatically.

The 95/95 Saver: The recycling of scrap metals goes back as far as 3,000 B.C. By recycling aluminum, we cut down on air pollution by 95 percent. And, we use 95 percent less energy recycling aluminum instead of using raw materials.